GET INTO ART

PEOPLE

SUSIE BROOKS

KINGFISHER

KINGFISHER

First published 2013 by Kingfisher
an imprint of Macmillan Children's Books
a division of Macmillan Publishers Limited
20 New Wharf Road, London N1 9RR
Basingstoke and Oxford
Associated companies throughout the world
www.panmacmillan.com

Edited by Catherine Brereton
Designed by Jane Tassie
Project photography by Geoff Dann

ISBN 978-0-7534-3577-9

9 8 7 6 5 4 3 2 1
1TR/0413/LFG/UG/140MA
A CIP catalogue record for this book is available from the British Library.
Printed in China

Picture credits
The Publisher would like to thank the following for permission to reproduce their
material. Every care has been taken to trace copyright holders. However, if there have
been unintentional omissions or failure to trace copyright holders, we apologize and
will, if informed, endeavour to make corrections in any future edition.

Cover and page 18 *A Sunday Afternoon on the Island of La Grande Jatte* by Georges
Seurat/Bridgeman Art Library/The Art Institute of Chicago; 6 *Vertumnus* by Giuseppe
Arcimboldo/AKG, London/IAM; 8 *Weeping Woman* by Pablo Picasso/Tate Images/Tate
Images; 10 *David* by Michelangelo Buonarroti/Getty Images/Bridgeman Art Library;
11 Art Archive/Galleria dell'Accademia, Venice; 12 *The Scream* by Edvard Munch/Art
Archive/Nasjonal Galleriet, Oslo; 14 *Children's Games* by Pieter Breugel the Elder/Bridgeman
Art Library/Kunsthistorisches Museum, Vienna; 16 *Portrait of Adele Bloch-Bauer I* by Gustav
Klimt/AKG, London/Erich Lessing; 20 *Grotesque Faces* by Leonardo da Vinci/Bridgeman
Art Library/Galleria dell'Accademia, Venice; 22 Corbis/Sandro Vannini; 24 *Girl in Mirror* by
Roy Lichtenstein/Bridgeman Art Library/Private Collection/Christie's Images; 26 *Lawn Tennis*
by Eadweard Muybridge/AKG, London/Collection Archiv fur Kunst & Geschichte, Berlin;
28 *Las Meninas* by Diego Velázquez/AKG, London/IAM.

CONTENTS

PICTURE A PERSON

Can you think of an art subject that's always around?
Just look in a mirror for the answer! Artists often base their work on themselves or other people. Some create portraits to remember people by, or characters to illustrate a story. Others capture feelings, actions, fashions or imaginary faces. The great thing is that people are all different and artists can bring them to life in many ways.

See how people have inspired famous artists –
then **let them inspire you too!** Each page of this book will tell you about a work of art and the person who created it. When you lift the flap, you'll find a project based on the artwork. Don't feel you have to copy it exactly. Half the fun of art is exploring your own ideas!

GETTING STARTED

There's a checklist on page 31 that will tell you what you need for each project, but it's a good idea to read through the steps before you begin. There are also some handy tips on the next page...

Always have a **pencil** and **rubber** handy. Making a rough **sketch** can help you plan a project and see how it's going to look.

PICK YOUR PAINT...

Acrylic paints are thick and bright – they're great for strong colours, or textures such as hair. **Ready-mix paints** are cheaper than acrylics but still bright. Use them when you need lots of paint.

Watercolours give a thinner colouring – try them over oil pastel or crayon, or draw on them in ink.

Use a mixture of thick and thin **paintbrushes**. Have a jam jar or plastic cup of water ready to rinse them in and a **palette** or paper plate for mixing paint.

TRY PASTELS...

Oil pastels have a bright, waxy look, like crayons. **Soft pastels** can be smudged and blended like chalk.

acrylic paint

Lay some newspaper on your surface before you start to paint!

watercolour paint

acrylic paint

sponged paint

soft pastel

oil pastels

For painting, use thick **cartridge** or **watercolour paper** – anything too thin will wrinkle. **Pastel paper** has a rough surface that holds on to the colour.

Collect a range of **coloured papers and card** for collage and 3-D models.

Look around at home for other art materials. Useful things include sponges, rags or cloths, cocktail sticks, drinking straws, scissors, glue, string, roller brushes and bubble wrap.

Ready to start?
Let's **get into**
art!

FOOD FEATURES

Experiment with fruits and vegetables to print some **foody figures!**

Cabbages and onions give a wrinkly effect.

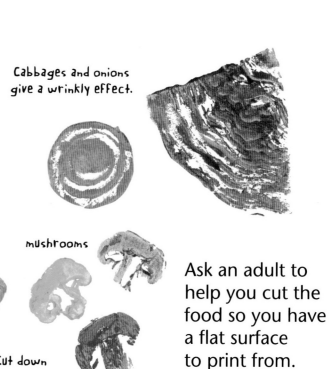

1 Ask if there are any spare fruits or vegetables in the kitchen. You don't need loads – you can cut them in different ways to print different shapes. Don't choose anything too juicy!

mushrooms

Ask an adult to help you cut the food so you have a flat surface to print from.

potato

Cut in half lengthways.

Cut across the middle.

carrot

Cut across the wide end.

Cut down the length.

2 Pat the food surface dry with kitchen paper, then use a paintbrush to cover it with paint. Press the paint down onto white paper. You can rinse the food if you want to change colour for the next print.

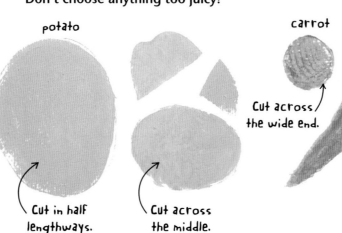

Cut thin strips of carrot for legs and arms like these.

Can you spot the prints of celery leaves and mushrooms in this picture?

broccoli

celery

red pepper

radish

potato

carrot

You could try using the colours of the vegetables themselves.

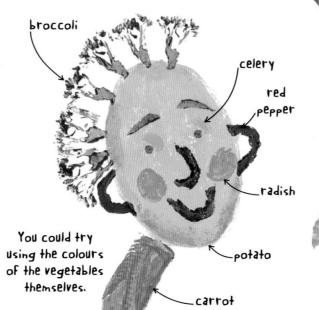

This figure has a red onion head, a pear body, celery arms, carrot legs and pepper hands, feet and hair!

Plants weren't the only things that Arcimboldo turned into heads. In a painting called *Air* he chose birds, *Earth* was a head made of animals, *The Cook* was a platter of meat and *The Librarian* was a pile of books. Some of his heads look like ordinary still lifes until you turn them upside down!

VERTUMNUS

Giuseppe Arcimboldo, *about* 1590

It could be a person – or a pile of fruits, vegetables and flowers!

Arcimboldo has cleverly mixed two sides of nature in this fascinating portrait of an emperor.

Plant person

Emperor Rudolf II was used to having his portrait painted – but not with pea-pod eyelids and a pear-shaped nose! Luckily he had a sense of humour, and he loved Arcimboldo's witty work. Here he is dressed up as Vertumnus, Roman god of the seasons. His face is recognizable, even though it's made up of plants!

Arcimboldo was a brilliant painter of nature. He also liked tricks and illusions. In this portrait he played with textures, painting lips as shiny cherries and a bristly sweet chestnut for a beard. One cheek is a rosy apple and the other a juicy peach. The ear is jokily shown as an ear of corn! What other fruits and vegetables can you see?

WHO WAS ARCIMBOLDO?

Giuseppe Arcimboldo was born in Italy in about 1526. He began his career designing cathedral windows, then went on to work for the imperial (royal) family in Austria. He designed costumes and festival sets and painted realistic portraits – but none of these had such an impact as his imaginative fruity heads!

FACE TO FACE

Use different viewpoints and bold shapes like Picasso's to make a face that's both **happy and sad!**

The lady in this painting is Picasso's girlfriend, Dora Maar. She's dressed in a hat, with neatly combed hair. Was she going out when she heard some bad news? Picasso made many paintings of her crying, at the time of the Spanish Civil War. He wanted to show the suffering that the war brought to so many people.

1 Cut out an oval head and neck shape from coloured paper. Draw around it on a different coloured paper and cut that out too.

2 Down the middle of one head, draw the side of a face with the nose and chin sticking out. Cut this out and glue it onto the other head.

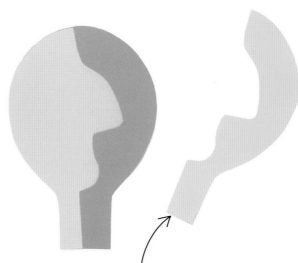

You could keep the spare piece to make another picture!

3 Glue the head onto a different coloured background, then start adding other features.

For hair, cut two wavy shapes, then cut one into narrow strips and stick them on.

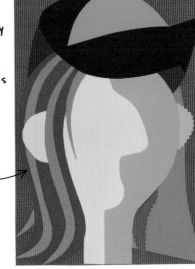

Add ears, and a hat if you like.

Try using zigzag craft scissors for some shapes.

4 When you add the eyes and mouth, think of one side being happy and the other sad. Show some parts facing forward and others to the side. If you want to include hands, do them last.

Use plenty of triangles and other geometric shapes.

WEEPING WOMAN

Pablo Picasso 1937

What's the first thing you notice about this picture? Probably that the woman is very sad. The way Picasso has painted her is strange and unrealistic, but it tells us exactly how she feels.

In pieces

Look at the shapes in the painting. They are sharp and jumbled, jabbing together in uncomfortable ways. The colours of the face are sickly, and in some places ghostly pale. A heavy tear cuts down the woman's cheek as she cries into a spiky handkerchief. An earring crushes her ear. She seems to be broken into pieces by sorrow.

Can you see how the mouth and nose point sideways, while the eyes stare straight ahead? Picasso liked to mix different viewpoints, as if we're looking from two directions at once. He could easily paint a realistic face – but he preferred to challenge our eyes!

WHO WAS PICASSO?

Pablo Picasso was born in Spain in 1881, the son of an art teacher. His first word was said to be 'piz' – short for lapiz, the Spanish for pencil! Picasso was a talented boy and grew up to be a great artist. He famously invented a style called Cubism, making pictures and sculptures from simplified shapes.

PERFECT PROPORTION

Whenever you **draw a face,** these rules will help you get it right!

Although Michelangelo knew about proportion, he made David's head, hands and upper body slightly too big. This may have been because the statue was meant to stand high up on Florence's cathedral. If people saw it from below, the proportions would seem correct!

1 Start with a simple upside-down egg shape. Dot a line lightly down the centre.

2 Measure halfway down the line and dot another line across. This is where the eyes go.

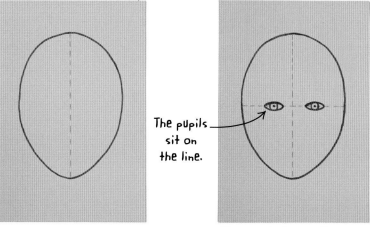

The pupils sit on the line.

The gap between the eyes is the same width as an eye.

3 Halfway between the eye line and the chin, draw another line. This is for the bottom of the nose and ears.

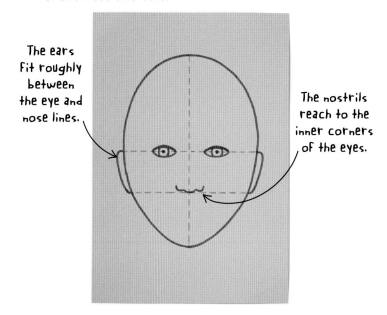

The ears fit roughly between the eye and nose lines.

The nostrils reach to the inner corners of the eyes.

4 Draw a final line halfway between the bottom of the nose and the chin. The mouth fits above this line.

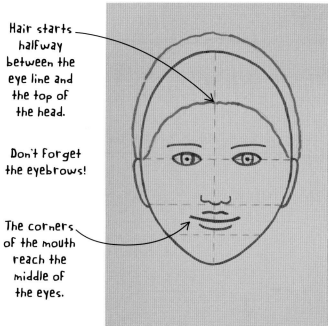

Hair starts halfway between the eye line and the top of the head.

Don't forget the eyebrows!

The corners of the mouth reach the middle of the eyes.

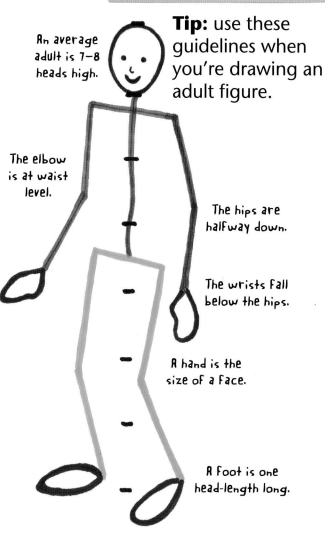

Tip: use these guidelines when you're drawing an adult figure.

An average adult is 7–8 heads high.

The elbow is at waist level.

The hips are halfway down.

The wrists fall below the hips.

A hand is the size of a face.

A foot is one head-length long.

DAVID

Michelangelo Buonarroti 1501–1504

Imagine a huge block of marble, taller than a double-decker bus.
That's what Michelangelo began with when he carved his statue of David! Nearly three years later it was complete.

Huge hero
Other artists had tried and failed to carve this enormous chunk of stone. But Michelangelo wasn't put off. He chipped away the marble to make a full human figure, about three times larger than life!

In the Bible story, David was a shepherd boy who killed the giant Goliath with a stone from his sling. These close-ups of the statue show his head and upper body. You can see he looks watchful and brave. His handsome face is evenly proportioned, his brow wrinkles thoughtfully, and veins and muscles bulge under his skin. Michelangelo has created the feel of real flesh, even though it's made of solid stone!

WHO WAS MICHELANGELO?

Michelangelo Buonarroti was born in Italy in 1475. Even as a boy, it was clear he would be a brilliant artist. He worked hard, studying anatomy to help him paint and sculpt the perfect human form. Michelangelo believed there was a statue in every block of stone – he just had to set it free!

THE SQUEAL

Create a happy version of Munch's painting!

3 Add ripples of colour around the figure. Smudge different colours together with your finger to blend them.

Try to cover all your pencil lines.

1 On a piece of rough-surfaced paper, draw a figure squealing with delight! Think about the pose and expression, but keep it simple.

Add a few background features, like a sun, fireworks or something that makes you happy.

Munch's style is called Expressionist because it expresses inner feelings, rather than a realistic view of the world. This figure looks neither male nor female – it's showing someone from the inside out. Munch made four versions of *The Scream* – two in pastel and two in paint. In 2012, one sold at auction for a record £74 million!

4 Carry on adding swirls of bright colour until your picture is complete.

2 Colour your figure with chalk or soft pastels. Use warm, bright colours like these.

Reds, oranges and yellows are warm, cheerful colours.

THE SCREAM

Edvard Munch 1893

If you could hear a painting, this one would hurt your ears! Munch has used bold colour and brushstrokes to put the piercing sound of a scream onto paper.

A scream of nature

The person in Munch's painting has a wide-open mouth – but that's not where the scream seems to come from. It's as if the sky and sea themselves are crying out, while the figure tries to block out the noise. Munch said that one day he 'sensed a great, infinite scream pass through nature' – and that's where he got the idea.

Look at the marks in the painting – they swirl and ripple like echoes. The sky is an angry, loud red and the water seems dark, deep and cold. Munch's figure looks ghostlike, swaying as if the scream is bouncing around inside. We get a sense of terror and confusion – which is just what the artist had felt.

WHO WAS MUNCH?

Edvard Munch was born in Norway in 1863. His mother and older sister died when he was young, and Edvard was often troubled by illness. He used art to show his feelings, but his pictures shocked many people at first. Eventually he found success and grew famous for his Expressionist style.

PLAYFUL POSES

You can paint a page of playful figures using a kitchen sponge!

1 Start by cutting out four shapes from the sponge.

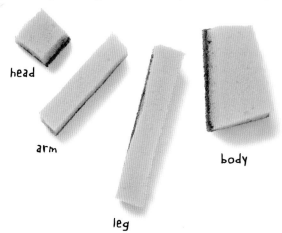

head

arm

leg

body

2 Practise printing on rough paper. Spread some thick paint onto a paper plate and dip in the sponge pieces one by one. Print the body first, then the head, legs and arms.

3 Now try printing several figures in a row, all in different poses.

You could use a fine paintbrush to add hair, hands or feet.

You can bend the arm and leg pieces as you print!

4 For your final painting, use a big sheet of paper or tape together some smaller ones. If you want to change the paint colour, rinse and squeeze dry the sponge bits, or cut some more.

Picture your figures **running, jumping** or **playing games.** Why not paint in a ball or a skipping rope!

CHILDREN'S GAMES

Pieter Bruegel the Elder 1560

Think of all the games you know – then imagine arranging them in one scene. When Bruegel made this picture he painted more than 200 children, playing in at least 80 different ways!

Old-fashioned fun

Games have changed a bit since Bruegel's time. Instead of modern toys, these children are playing with sticks, hoops, stones and barrels. But you might recognize some activities – like leapfrog, hide and seek and blind man's buff. Can you see two boys on stilts, someone blowing bubbles, and a girl on a hobby horse?

Bruegel loved painting lots of little figures together. He arranged them carefully, leading our eye to every part of the scene. Each child is in a different pose, and the high viewpoint means that every single person can be seen.

WHO WAS BRUEGEL?

Pieter Brueghel was a Flemish artist, born in about 1525. He dropped the 'h' from his name and became known as 'the Elder' to distinguish himself from his two painter sons. In Bruegel's time, artists often painted idealized scenes. But he preferred to show the reality of ordinary peasant life.

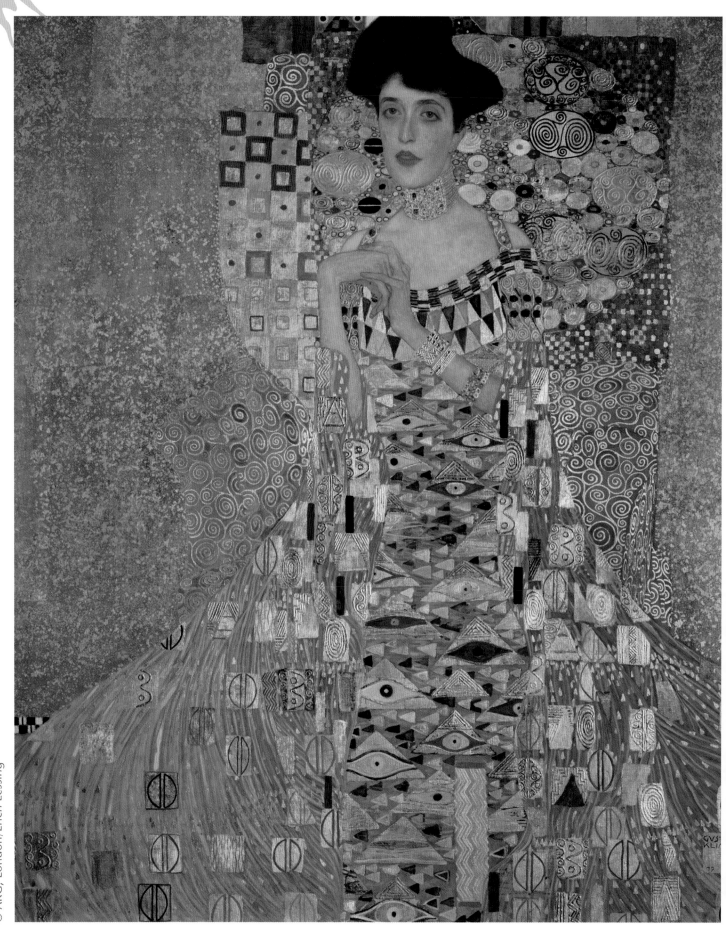

PATCHWORK PATTERNS

Practise different ways of **making Klimt-style patterns and textures.**

1 Scratch patterns into wet acrylic paint…

with a plastic fork

with the end of a paintbrush

with a drinking straw

2 Lay paper onto different textures and rub with a crayon.

net food bag

polystyrene pizza tray

wicker basket or chair

grater

3 Tear or scrunch tissue paper and glue it in a pattern onto card.

4 Make prints from different objects…

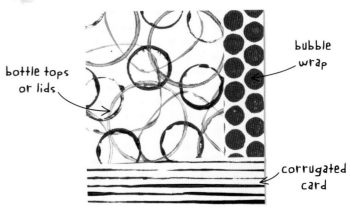

bottle tops or lids

bubble wrap

corrugated card

5 Print from cling film, or lay cling film onto wet ink or watercolour and peel it off when dry.

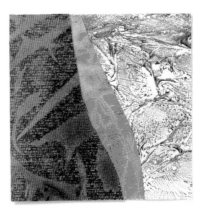

6 Draw a pattern in oil pastel, then paint over it with watercolour paint.

You get this speckled effect by sprinkling salt on the wet paint and brushing it off when the paint dries.

Can you design a costume using your patterns? Try arranging them into a shape, such as this hat.

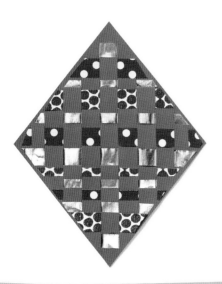

Klimt made more studies for this painting than any other in his career. A study is a rough drawing or painting that helps an artist to plan a piece of work. Klimt made many sketches in chalk or charcoal, playing around with different poses and exploring the decoration of Adele's gown.

PORTRAIT OF ADELE BLOCH-BAUER I

Gustav Klimt 1907

Not many people have their portraits made in gold, but Adele Bloch-Bauer was a wealthy lady!
Klimt borrowed ideas from mosaics he'd seen in Italy to create this luxurious picture.

Gleaming glamour

It was Adele's husband who commissioned the portrait – he was a fan of Klimt's work and he had plenty of money to spend on it. The gold you see here isn't paint but gold leaf – thin, fragile sheets of real gold. As Klimt stuck it to his canvas, it wrinkled into beautiful textures.

Klimt used oil paint for the figure and the colours in her decorative dress. He loved to play with patterns and shapes, arranged in a detailed patchwork style. Working like this was slow, and the portrait took nearly three years. But Klimt didn't mind – he enjoyed painting this glamorous lady!

WHO WAS KLIMT?

Gustav Klimt was born in Austria in 1862, the son of a gold engraver. He began his career painting murals and decorative ceilings. Later he became known for his pictures of women. His unusual, ornamental style broke away from the traditional art of his time.

SUNNY SPOTS

Where would you like to be on a sunny Sunday? **Say it in spots!**

3 Gradually add dots of other colours. Wipe the rubber with a damp cloth when you change paint colours.

For light areas, dot white paint on and around the colour.

For shadows, add dots of dark or contrasting colours.

1 Sketch out a simple scene on a piece of thick white paper. Don't make it too big or it will take ages to paint.

Keep the figures simple. If you draw them from the back, you won't need to do their faces!

For water, use dark and light blues and white. Add dots of colour for reflections.

4 Keep adding dots until you've finished your scene!

2 Pick a paint colour to start with and squeeze some onto a palette. Use the rubber on the end of a pencil to dot the paint onto the page.

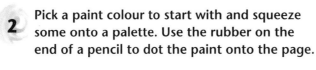

Think about the colours you use to paint the figures. Light colours stand out against darker ones. Contrasting colours zing out too.

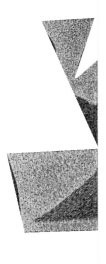

A SUNDAY AFTERNOON
ON THE ISLAND OF LA GRANDE JATTE

Georges Seurat 1884

If you're seeing spots, you're not going dotty – Seurat built up this whole scene using multicoloured specks of paint!

Colour clever

Hold the painting away from you – it's hard to see the dots from afar. That's what Seurat wanted. His idea was to let our eyes blend the colours, instead of mixing them on a palette. He thought this made everything look brighter.

Seurat placed his dots carefully, using contrasting colours to make different areas stand out. The figures look almost like cut-outs. There's a lot of action, but everything seems still, as if someone has pressed pause in a movie. This gives us the feel of a relaxing Sunday afternoon.

WHO WAS SEURAT?

Georges Seurat was born in France in 1859. He studied art, and also the science of colour and light – that's how he developed his style, known as Pointillism. At first people criticized his work, but this giant painting changed their minds!

Leonardo's sketches were a bit like early cartoons. **Try doodling your own**

FUNNY FACES

An open mouth and raised eyebrow give a shocked expression.

1 Start with just lines. Think about different expressions and how the eyes, eyebrows and mouth change. Experiment with different shaped noses, chins, ears and hair!

Downward sloping eyebrows look cross.

Curve the mouth upwards and widen the eye for a happy face.

2 If you want to add shading, try using watery paint or ink.

3 Now draw some outlines on coloured or patterned paper. Stick them onto card, then cut them out and make them into lolly stick puppets!

A round mouth looks puzzled or surprised.

Glue or tape the stick to the back of the card head.

Leonardo made these sketches in brown ink on paper. He was always scribbling in notebooks, recording his ideas. Usually he wrote backwards in mirror writing! This was probably because he was left-handed, and it was easier to move his pen from right to left without smudging the ink.

GROTESQUE FACES

Leonardo da Vinci 16th century

Are these people real or imaginary? Probably a bit of both! Leonardo has combined mis-shapen chins and noses with funny expressions in this set of strange-looking characters.

Ugly but interesting

Leonardo was obsessed by faces. He filled whole sketchbooks with pages like this and made notes about different features. For example, a nose could be straight, bulbous, hollow, pointed… the list went on! Can you think of ways he might have described eyes, mouths, chins and necks too?

Leonardo would search the streets for unusual faces to draw. Sometimes he followed people all day then made sketches later. Most of his 'grotesques' show old men or women with sagging skin and toothless jaws. They nearly all face sideways, as if they don't know they're being watched.

WHO WAS LEONARDO?

Leonardo da Vinci was born in Italy in 1452. He lived during the Renaissance, when a lot of great art was being made. Leonardo was a scientist, inventor, writer, architect, musician, mathematician and all-round genius as well as being a brilliant artist! He was curious about everything, and it showed in all his work.

© Corbis/Sandro Vannini

MUMMY MASK

To preserve their dead, the Egyptians bandaged them as mummies – but first, they removed certain body parts and kept them in four jars. These jars showed the heads of the Four Sons of Horus, who you can see at the bottom of the mask above. The falcon-headed gods at either side of his sons represent Horus himself.

For a quicker version of this project, miss out step 2 and just use paint for the face and other decoration.

1 On the back of a paper plate, draw an Egyptian-style face, with wide, heavily outlined eyes. Then draw around the plate on a big piece of cardboard and cut out a headdress shape like this.

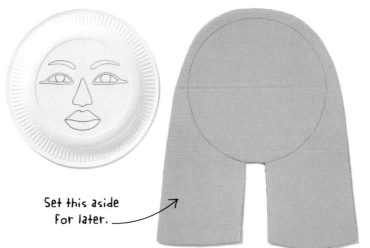

Set this aside for later.

2 Now you'll need some white craft glue with a nozzle top. Practise squeezing lines of it on scrap paper, then go over the outlines on your plate. Leave it to dry overnight or until the glue is hard.

The glue will probably dry clear.

While you're waiting, you could make some decorations for the headdress (see step 4).

3 When the glue is dry, cover the face with gold or yellow acrylic paint.

Add some colour to the eyes, eyebrows and mouth.

4 Let the paint dry, then glue the plate to the headdress. Decorate the mask with bits of shiny paper or your own painted designs.

You can cover the rim of the plate or paint it as part of the design.

These lumpy bits were done with glue, as in step 2.

Tip: If you don't have metallic paper, try colouring kitchen foil with felt pens!

EGYPTIAN BURIAL MASK

Ancient Egyptian craftsmen, *around* 3000BCE to 1st century CE

This might seem an elaborate way to dress up a dead person – but in ancient Egypt, looking good after death was important!

Forever face

The Egyptians believed that when you died, you could live on forever in the afterlife. To get there, your body had to be preserved so your soul always had a home – and a burial mask helped with this. It meant your soul could recognize your body, and it also gave protection in the tomb.

The type of mask depended a lot on how rich or important you were. If you were royal, it was made of gold and jewels! The main mask shown here was painted gold, for a woman who had less money. Around her face is a patterned headdress, decorated with symbols of the afterlife. The black, jackal-headed figures are the god Anubis, who was known as protector of the dead.

HOW WERE THEY MADE?

Masks like this were usually made of cartonnage – a material a bit like paper maché. They began as a mould, or cast, of the person's face. This was then painted with an idealized image, rather than an accurate portrait. Gold was often used because it was the colour of the flesh of the gods.

DOTTY DAZZLER

For this project, **imagine you're creating a close-up in a film or comic strip**. What is your character doing or thinking? Make a sketch first if you like.

Lichtenstein wanted to give his work the mechanical feel of mass printing. He chose only the colours used in industrial printing: red, yellow, blue and black on white. To create his dots, he painted through rows of holes in a metal screen. This picture is done on steel and is over a metre square.

1 To make some Ben-Day dots, spread paint over a sheet of bubble wrap using a sponge or roller. Lay a piece of white paper on top and press firmly, then peel it off.

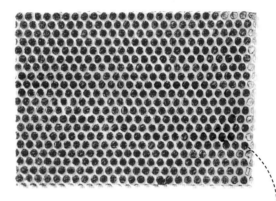

You can fill in any uneven bits with a paintbrush.

2 When the dots are dry, cut out a face. It doesn't have to be a whole face – draw it coming off the edge of the page. Then lay it on some coloured paper and draw hair around it.

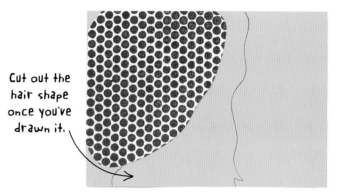

Cut out the hair shape once you've drawn it.

3 Glue the face and hair onto a coloured background. Cut out eyes, a mouth and any other details and stick them on.

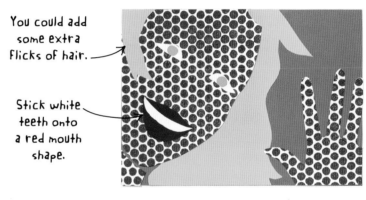

You could add some extra flicks of hair.

Stick white teeth onto a red mouth shape.

4 Finish off your picture with a marker pen or black paint. Add eyebrows, a nose and a thick outline around all the shapes.

Try sticking on a window frame like this.

GIRL IN MIRROR

Roy Lichtenstein 1964

Every picture tells a story – especially if it's in a comic strip!

Lichtenstein loved the way that comics put drama on a page, so he copied their style in his paintings.

Painting like print

Are you wondering why this girl is spotty? She hasn't really got spots! Lichtenstein borrowed a technique used in printing, called Ben-Day dots. Rows of these dots would make up different colours in a comic strip. Lichtenstein created his own version on a much bigger scale.

Notice the thick black outlines in the painting. They are typical of comics too. So is the way that Lichtenstein cropped the girl's head in close-up. Because we see just one isolated scene, we have to imagine the story. Where is she going? What is she thinking? Who is she trying to impress?

WHO WAS LICHTENSTEIN?

Roy Lichtenstein was born in the USA in 1923. He studied and taught art and tried out many styles, but it was Pop Art that made him famous. He took the bold, brash images of advertising and print and turned them into valuable paintings. Glamorous comic-book blondes were one of his favourite subjects.

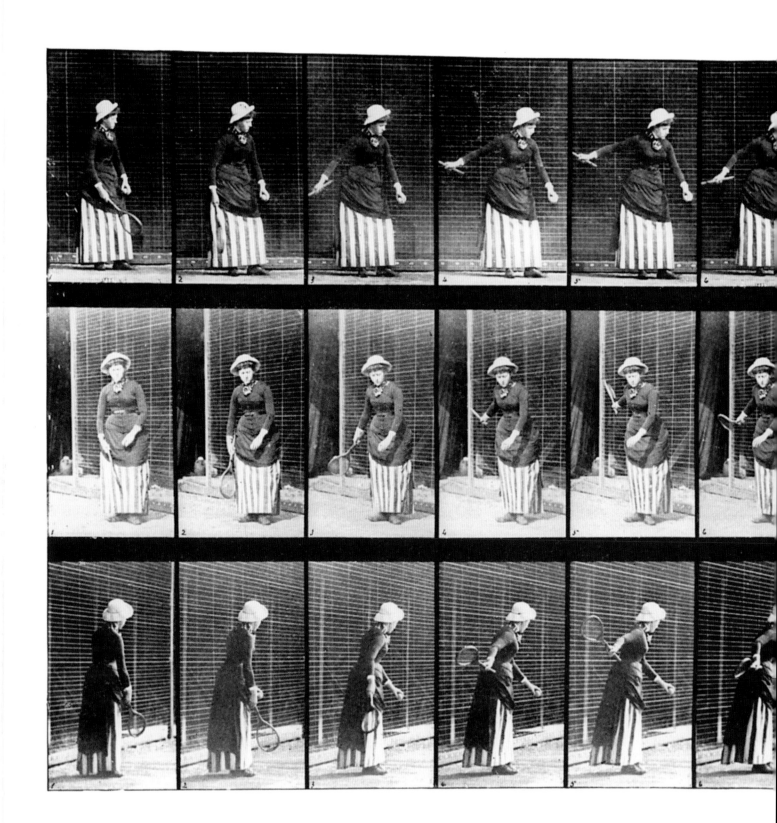

ACTION SNAPS

To photograph your own action sequences you'll need **a camera** and **a friend**.

1 Decide what movement you are going to photograph. It's best if it's something that can be done slowly. Get your friend to try moving in slow motion and holding each stage of the pose.

When you're ready to start, stand at a good distance from your subject so he or she fills the camera frame.

2 Keep the same distance between you and your friend as you photograph each stage of the action. If your model moves in one direction, you should move, too.

3 If you're photographing something quick, like a somersault, get your friend to repeat the move and press the shutter button at a different stage each time.

4 Print out your photos and arrange them in sequence, or 'stitch' them together on a computer.

LAWN TENNIS

Eadweard Muybridge 1887

These photos aren't frames from a movie – they were taken with lots of still cameras! Muybridge has captured the many stages of a movement, so it slowly unwinds before our eyes.

Fast photographs

In Muybridge's day, photography was very new. Few people had tackled moving subjects before. Muybridge developed a fast-shutter camera that would capture movement without blurring. He sometimes lined up 24 of these cameras to shoot an action sequence!

Muybridge photographed this woman playing tennis from three angles at once. We can see her from the side, front and back as she swings her racket. Look down each column and you'll notice she's in the same position. Look along each row and you'll see how the racket moves. Muybridge invented a machine called a zoopraxiscope to 'play' his photos quickly one after the other. It made the pictures seem to move.

WHO WAS MUYBRIDGE?

Eadweard Muybridge was born in 1830 in England, but he lived mainly in the USA. His first action photos were of a galloping horse – to settle a bet that all of its feet left the ground at the same time!

© AKG, London/IAM

MY FAMILY

Imagine a snapshot of life in your home.
Put yourself in the picture
with this fun family collage!

1 First do a rough sketch of your scene. Who's there and what are they up to?

brother playing with friends

mum chatting

sister dancing

something cooking

me drawing

dad snoring

When an artist paints a picture of him or herself, it's called a self-portrait. This one shows us how Velázquez worked, standing at an easel with a wooden palette in one hand. The canvas he is painting is huge – just like *Las Meninas*, which is over 3 metres tall and nearly 3 metres wide!

2 Now take a large piece of paper and stick down the background. You could use scraps of craft paper, wrapping paper, wallpaper or even paint your own.

white paint sponged onto blue paper

torn green paper for the grass

3 Put together your figures and other details. Look through magazines for different colours and textures to use. Cut out shapes and glue them together.

Cut hair from a hair photo.

Cut out a skin-coloured face and draw or stick on eyes, nose, mouth and ears.

Try a photo of a carpet for pet fur!

4 Glue everything onto your scene.

LAS MENINAS

Diego Velázquez 1656

Sometimes there's more to a painting than first meets the eye – and you need to look carefully at this one! Velázquez has cleverly woven in an extra subject. Can you spot what it is?

Double vision

Who is the first person you notice? Probably the blonde girl in the centre. She is a princess, and the others are her *meninas*, or maids of honour. One of the girls seems to be handing her a drink. But are they the main subject of the portrait? Look again.

To the left of the scene we see an artist – Velázquez himself. He's not painting the princess, but he is gazing towards us just as she is. Who or what are they looking at? The clue is in the background. On the wall there is a mirror, and in it is the reflection of two people – the king and queen! We see the scene from their viewpoint. It's as if a moment in the royal household has been frozen in time.

WHO WAS VELÁZQUEZ?

Diego Velázquez was born in Spain in 1599. By the age of 11 he knew he wanted to be an artist. In his twenties he became official painter to King Philip IV of Spain, whose family we see in this portrait. The king gave Velázquez a home in his palace so he could paint for him all the time!

ART WORDS AND INFO

anatomy The way a living thing is built. In humans this includes bones, muscles and other inside parts.

auction A sale where people bid for items, and the bidder offering the highest price wins.

canvas A strong type of fabric that artists can paint on.

carve To shape something by cutting into it. An artist may carve wood, stone or other materials to make a sculpture.

collage A picture made by sticking pieces of paper, fabric or other objects onto a background.

commission To pay someone to create a particular item, such as a portrait.

contrasting (or complementary) colours Colours that are opposite each other on the colour wheel. If you place contrasting colours next to each other, they stand out more.

Cubism (1907–1920s) An art style in which artists including Picasso made images using simple geometric shapes.

Expressionist Linked to the art style Expressionism (1905–1920s). Expressionist artists wanted to show emotion through their work, often using exaggerated shapes or colours.

geometric shape A recognized mathematical shape, such as a triangle.

gold leaf Gold that is beaten out into very thin, delicate sheets and used for decoration.

idealized Shown in an ideal or unnaturally perfect form.

illusion Something that seems to be one thing when it's actually another.

imperial Relating to an empire or its royal rulers, called emperors.

COLOUR CONNECTIONS

In art there are three primary colours – **red**, **yellow** and **blue**. These are colours that can't be mixed from any others. Each primary colour has an opposite, or complementary, that is made by mixing the other two.

If you mix a colour with its complementary, you'll get a shade of brown.

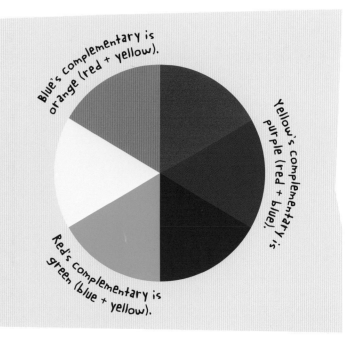

Blue's complementary is orange (red + yellow).

Yellow's complementary is purple (red + blue).

Red's complementary is green (blue + yellow).

mosaic A design made up of small pieces of glass, tile or other material, stuck onto a surface.

mural A picture that's painted straight onto a wall.

Pointillism (mid 1880s–1890s) Also called Divisionism. A style of painting using dots of unmixed colour that blend together when seen from a distance.

Pop Art (mid 1950s–1960s) An art style that celebrated the bold, bright images of advertising, cartoon strips and popular entertainment.

print A way of transferring an image from one surface to another. For example, a design may be scratched into metal, then covered with paint or ink. When this is pressed onto paper, it produces a negative, or reverse, image that can be reproduced many times.

proportion The balance of parts in a whole – for example the size of someone's head in relation to their body.

Renaissance (1300s–1500s) A time in European history when there were great developments in art and culture, often based on Classical ideas from ancient Greece and Rome.

sculpture Three-dimensional art. Carving and clay modelling are both types of sculpture. Someone who does this is called a sculptor.

still life An arrangement of objects, such as a bowl of fruit or flowers, set up for an artist to paint or photograph.

texture The feel of a surface, such as rough fabric or smooth skin.

PROJECT CHECKLIST

These are the materials you'll need for each project. The ones in brackets are useful but you can manage without!

Food features (page 7) fruits and vegetables, knife, kitchen paper, paintbrush, acrylic or ready-mix paints, paper plate or palette, thick white paper

Face to face (page 9) different coloured papers, pencil, scissors, glue, (zigzag craft scissors)

Perfect proportion (page 11) paper, pencil or pen

The Squeal (page 13) rough-surfaced paper, pencil, soft pastels or chalk

Playful poses (page 15) kitchen sponge, scissors, acrylic or ready-mix paints, paper plate or palette, coloured paper, paintbrush, (sticky tape)

Patchwork patterns (page 17) acrylic, ready-mix and watercolour paints, ink, paper plate or palette, crayons, oil pastels, coloured papers, tissue paper, scissors, glue, paintbrushes, scratchers (eg plastic fork, drinking straw), textured surfaces (eg pizza tray, corrugated card, bubble wrap), cling film, salt

Sunny spots (page 19) thick white paper, pencil with a rubber on the end, acrylic or ready-mix paints, paper plate or palette, damp cloth

Funny faces (page 21) paper, pencils or pens, watercolour paint or ink, patterned papers, card, scissors, glue, lolly sticks, (sticky tape)

Mummy mask (page 23) paper plate, pencil, thick cardboard, scissors, white craft glue with nozzle top, scrap paper, acrylic paints (including gold), paintbrush, paper plate or palette, shiny coloured paper (or kitchen foil and felt pens)

Dotty dazzler (page 25) bubble wrap, sponge or roller, acrylic or ready-mix paint, paper plate or palette, white paper, scissors, coloured paper, pencil, glue, black marker pen (or paintbrush and black paint)

Action snaps (page 27) camera, friend, computer, (printer, paper, scissors, glue)

My family (page 29) large sheet of paper, pencil, coloured paper, patterned papers, magazines, (paint, paper plate or palette, sponge), scissors, glue

INDEX